Presented To

Presented By

Date

meditations & prayers
to bring you closer to God

PRAYER
Moments
FOR MOMS

Ψ
inspirio

Prayer Moments for Moms
ISBN 0-310-80492-2

Published by Inspirio™, The gift group of Zondervan
5300 Patterson Avenue, SE
Grand Rapids, Michigan 49530

Requests for information should be addressed to:
Inspirio™, The gift group of Zondervan
Grand Rapids, Michigan 49530
http://www.inspiriogifts.com

Editor: Lila Empson
Project Manager: Tom Dean
Writer: Sherry A. Morris
Design: Whisner Design Group, Tulsa, Oklahoma

Printed in China.

04 05 06 / 4 3 2 1

As a mother comforts her child,
so will I comfort you.

Isaiah 66:13 NIV

Contents

Teach children how they should live, and they will remember it all their life.

Proverbs 22:6 GNT

Introduction

Prayer begins a relationship with God. From heaven, God reaches down for a hand that reaches up to hold his in childlike faith. As a mother reaches for God's hand in prayer, she learns from him how to be a loving parent. As she is comforted, she learns to comfort. As she receives God's patient discipline, she learns to discipline likewise. Becoming a praying child of God gives a mother the wisdom she needs to be a godly parent.

Walking hand in hand with a child of her own also helps a mother understand God's love. Through loving, caring for, and making the best choices for her child, she comes to a better understanding of how God could always have in mind what is best for his children. Nurturing her own children helps a mother's faith to grow.

With trusting eyes, a mother can look to God and know that she is loved. She'll find him looking back with amazing tenderness. A prayer is all that's needed to take a mother to his waiting arms of love.

A MOM'S
Job

Almighty God, heavenly Father, you have blessed
us with the joy and care of children: Give us calm
strength and patient wisdom as we bring them up,
that we may teach them to love whatever is just
and true and good, following the example of our
Savior Jesus Christ. Amen.

∞

The Book of Common Prayer

Let us boldly approach the throne of grace. . . .
We will find grace to help us when we need it.

   Hebrews 4:16 NIrV

Just Ask

"My umbrella is gone," four-year-old Amy cried. Amy and her mother, Roz, searched through all the rain gear outside the door of the Sunday-school classroom, but to no avail. Amy's prized birthday gift was gone.

On the way home from church, Roz asked her still tearful daughter, "Did you ask God to help you find your umbrella?"

Roz wasn't sure if her suggestion to say a prayer for a lost umbrella wasn't just setting Amy up for a big disappointment. But the look on Amy's face warmed Roz's heart.

"I'll ask God to help me find it, every day until I do!" Amy exclaimed.

Continue to grow in the grace and knowledge of our Lord.

2 Peter 3:18 GNT

Every week at church Amy asked hopefully about her umbrella. Each night at bedtime she petitioned earnestly in prayer. For five weeks she continued to pray.

One Sunday morning, Amy burst

out of her classroom shouting, "Mama, Mama, look what God did for me!" She ran to her parents with a big smile and her lost umbrella.

As Roz saw the joy on her little girl's face, she could almost see God smiling too. "Did you ask?" was the question that led to an answered prayer. *Maybe the size of the problem doesn't matter,* she thought for the first time. *Maybe we just need to ask.*

Though not every prayer is answered the way you might expect, each time you pray God teaches you something about his goodness. You can approach the throne of grace with confidence knowing that he hears and answers your prayers.

In everything, by prayer and petition, with thanksgiving, present your requests to God. And the peace of God . . . will guard your hearts and your minds in Christ Jesus.
Philippians 4:6–7 NIV

God, help me to ask with a faith that expects to proclaim, "Look what God did for me."
Amen.

How great is the love the Father has lavished on us, that we should be called children of God!

1 John 3:1 NIV

God's Child

Pamela was only eighteen months old when her father, Richard, an officer in the army, left to fight in World War II. For Pamela's mother, Dorlene, evenings were lonely and difficult. Her heart ached for herself— and for Pamela. Would her tiny daughter ever know her father, or would she only remember him as a picture on the dresser by her bed? Through the long months of waiting, Dorlene welcomed the nightly ritual of tucking her little girl into bed. Each night they kissed Richard's picture and prayed that God would bring him safely home.

When the war was over, Pamela was four years old. Dorlene took her to the train station to meet Richard as he came home for the first time in almost three years. They stood on the platform along with a mass of other families waiting for their special soldiers. The terminal was a sea of uniforms. Suddenly Pamela screamed, "Daddy!" and ran toward her father

There is nothing in all creation that will ever be able to separate us from the love of God.

Romans 8:39 GNT

with open arms. Although she had been just a baby when he left, she recognized him from the picture she kissed each night. Richard scooped her up with hugs and kisses.

"Do you know me?" she asked him hopefully.

"Of course I know you," he smiled through his tears. "You're my little girl."

Nothing can ever separate you from God's love. You can be assured that your God will not ever forget you, no matter what. Each time you run to him in prayer, he will open his arms and say, "Of course I know you! You're my little girl."

You love him, although you have not seen him, and you believe in him, although you do not now see him. So you rejoice with a great and glorious joy which words cannot express.

1 Peter 1:8 GNT

God, thank you that I can always be assured you are waiting for me to run to you.

Amen.

*Trust in the LORD with all your heart
and lean not on your own understanding.*

Proverbs 3:5 NIV

Igniting Faith

In *Anna and the King,* Anna attempted to teach the physical reality of scientific principles to her young Burmese students. She placed a peeled boiled egg on top of a bottle and asked the children if they believed the egg could go into the bottle without first breaking up. Because the egg was too big to fit through the bottle's opening, the children reasoned that no, it could not. Anna ignited a piece of paper and threw it into the bottle. Because the fire used up all the oxygen inside the bottle, a vacuum was created that pulled the flexible egg inside. The children were amazed.

Anna, like any good teacher, knew that the children needed to see the scientific principles at work to understand.

If we ask anything in keeping with what he wants, he hears us.

1 John 5:14 NIrV

All God's children have a great Teacher who helps them understand how his power works within them. Just as trying to fit an egg into a bottle seems impossible at first, finding answers to some challenges can seem beyond our imagination. But igniting a prayer of faith releases God's power to shape his children's will to fit his plan. When our prayers are in keeping with what he wants, nothing is impossible.

∽

Like a wide-eyed child is astonished to discover that an egg can fit into a bottle, you will be amazed to see the the power of God at work in your life. In the classroom of prayer, God is a patient teacher helping you open the eyes of your heart and believe.

God is able to do far more than we could ever ask for or imagine. He does everything by his power that is working in us.
Ephesians 3:20 NIrV

God, may my prayers ignite sparks of faith that release your power to work in me.
Amen.

Then you, your children and their children after them will have respect for the LORD your God as long as you live.

Deuteronomy 6:2 NIrV

Tucked-in Memories

"Mom," said seventeen-year-old Kellibeth, "Do you remember the prayer you used to pray when you tucked me in at night?"

"Well, let me think a minute," her mother answered. "Didn't it go something like, 'Thank you, God, for Kellibeth, and please bless her and keep her safe tonight. Thank you for loving Kellibeth and for giving her the gift of Jesus.' "

"That was it."

"Why do you ask?"

"My friend and I were talking about when we learned to pray. She didn't learn to pray until she was older. I told her how I couldn't fall asleep until you came to pray with me. Then I would fall asleep telling God what was on my mind. Though I didn't understand who Jesus was exactly, I felt I must be very special if God had given me Jesus for a gift.

I pray that Christ will make his home in your hearts through faith.

Ephesians 3:17 GNT

And if I was scared, I just remembered that God loved me and would keep me safe. I felt very secure."

"Thanks, honey, for sharing that with me. Do you think you'll tuck your children in with a prayer?"

"Yes, I do. And thanks, mom, for setting an example for me."

⌒⌒

Just like taking a warm bath or reading a bedtime story, praying can be part of a nightly routine that gives a small child comfort and security before falling asleep. The gift of prayer wrapped in sweet memories can be a precious legacy to tuck into your children's hearts.

Put into practice what you learned and received from me, both from my words and from my actions. And the God who gives us peace will be with you.
Philippians 4:9 GNT

God, let the gift of prayer be a legacy in our family that lasts for many generations.
Amen.

PRAYER
Heart of Wisdom

Lord, make a channel of Thy peace,

that where there is hatred I may bring love;

That where there is wrong,

I may bring the spirit of forgiveness;

That where there is doubt, I may bring faith;

That where there is error, I may bring truth;

That where there is discord, I may bring harmony;

That where there is despair, I may bring hope;

That where there are shadows, I may bring light; That

where there is sadness, I may bring joy.

MOTHER TERESA

18

We pray this in order that you may live a life worthy of the Lord and may please him in every way: bearing fruit in every good work, growing in the knowledge of God.

Colossians 1:10 NIV

THE MOTHER'S HEART IS THE
CHILD'S SCHOOLROOM.

HENRY WARD BEECHER

The wisdom that comes from heaven is first of all pure; then peace–loving, considerate, submissive, full of mercy and good fruit, impartial and sincere.

James 3:17 NIV

The LORD will watch over your coming and going both now and forevermore.

Psalm 121:8 NIV

Under the Covers

"Grandma," said Debbie, "I want the pink comforter."

Grandma pulled the once thick, slightly frayed comforter from the closet and spread it over the bed. "Are you afraid to sleep by yourself?" she asked her granddaughter.

"No," Debbie replied. "I'll be all right."

Grandma said prayers with Debbie and turned out the light. "I'll leave the hall light on for you," she said as she blew another kiss goodnight.

Debbie snuggled deeper into the four-poster bed. She covered up her head, and true to her words, fell right to sleep.

I will lie down and sleep in peace. LORD, you alone keep me safe.

Psalm 4:8 NIrV

What a change, thought Grandma. *Only a few months ago she wouldn't even go to sleep unless I stayed with her.* The comforter had made all the difference.

One night Debbie was having her usual trouble falling asleep. Grandma found the old, pink comforter and spread it over Debbie and the big bed. "This is the comforter your mother slept under when she was a little girl," she told the tearful child. "It made her feel safe."

The next morning a happy little girl awoke and asked for breakfast.

"Did you sleep well?" Grammy asked.

"Of course," Debbie answered. "I was under my comforter."

∞

Prayer is like a comforter, spread over your life. Just as a child feels secure after being tucked in with a favorite blanket, you can have the sweet assurance that God is covering you with his hand of protection, watching over you day and night.

Give praise to the God and Father of our Lord Jesus Christ! He is the Father who gives tender love. All comfort comes from him.
2 Corinthians 1:3 NIrV

Thank you, God, that you tenderly spread your comforter of protection over me.
Amen.

I will praise the LORD, who counsels me;
even at night my heart instructs me.

Psalm 16:7 NIV

Your Own Special Song

Kathy sat on the back porch hoping to find a few minutes of respite in the quiet of a spring night. At first the minutes seemed filled with the peacefulness that comes from a lack of human voices, but gradually the night noises pervaded her senses. The sound of cars on a distant street, the wail of a train whistle, and the muffled beat of music from the television in the den created a discordant harmony against the serene natural melody made by cicadas and tree frogs.

Listening intently, she began to discern other sounds—birds calling to each other in the branches above her, an animal scurrying through the grasses just outside the fence, and the gentle rustling of trees stirred by the wind. *The sounds that God made are all I want to hear tonight,* she thought. *His nighttime symphony quiets my heart like nothing else.* She settled a little deeper into the lawn chair and focused on listening only to the resplendent music of God's creation.

By day the LORD directs his love, at night his song is with me.

Psalm 42:8 NIV

22

Soon she filtered out the harsh man-made sounds and attuned her ears only to nature. An audience of one under the starlit sky, Kathy enjoyed the calming music and said a prayer of thanks to the composer.

Listening to God is like discerning the many sounds of a spring night. His is the voice of love that can be heard apart from all the others. What a joy it is to know God speaks when his children pause to listen and to feel the quiet of his love.

The LORD will take great delight in you, he will quiet you with his love, he will rejoice over you with singing.
Zephaniah 3:17 NIV

God, may I find those quiet moments and listen to your special song of love for me. Amen.

Amazing Grace

Knowing that money was tight and she needed to find a part-time job soon, Janet wondered how she'd manage to care for her children and work, too. Then Janet's old boss called, offering her a part-time project. If she could meet the client for lunch, the job was hers.

Getting an infant and toddler ready took more time than she had thought. In her rush to get out the door, she left the scribbled note with the restaurant's address behind. *Where's the restaurant?* She was frantic when she realized she'd left her cell phone in the diaper bag at the sitter's. Time was running out. *Dear God, if this is the right job for me, please give me grace to get there on time. Help me find a gas station with a phone book.*

Just then her eyes caught sight of a phone book's flapping pages on the side of the road. Not quite believing her eyes, Janet pulled over, picked up the phone book that was lying on the ground, and looked up the address.

After a successful meeting with the client, Janet prayed, *Thank you, God, for helping me to see that even if things don't always go smoothly, your grace is still sufficient for me.*

∽

Though you can't be certain what each day holds, you can know that God is sufficient to meet your needs and carry you through. Not every day brings small miracles like a phone book by the side of the road, but God can help you through challenges and supply your needs through his amazing grace.

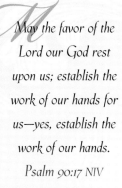

May the favor of the Lord our God rest upon us; establish the work of our hands for us—yes, establish the work of our hands.

Psalm 90:17 NIV

God, thank you that you already know what's going to happen today and will supply my needs with grace that is sufficient for me.
Amen.

Knock and the door will be opened to you.

Luke 11:9 NIV

Rock, Paper, Scissors

No matter where they went, Virgie's three boys ran out the back door of the house to the car yelling and arguing. "It's my turn to sit up front!" each one yelled. One day in desperation, Virgie said a prayer, which was followed immediately by a moment of inspiration: Play rock, paper, scissors.

In this childhood game, rock beats scissors, scissors cut paper, paper covers rock. Rock, paper, and scissors each have their own gesture that has to be made simultaneously between players. Last person standing wins.

Elijah won. "Okay," said their mother firmly. "Elijah, you get to choose. You can choose for one of your brothers to sit in the front seat, or you can take the seat yourself."

The Lord gives wisdom, and from his mouth come knowledge and understanding.

Proverbs 2:6 NIV

"Are we going to do this every time?" Elijah asked.

"If you take the seat now, you won't play next time. Your brothers will play to see who gets to ride up front next. Whoever is beaten then will be the last one to ride up front. Then it will be fair. Everyone will be sure to get a turn."

"I guess that's fair," Elijah admitted meekly.

Virgie thanked God for sudden moments of inspiration.

Sometimes you need to pause to ask for wisdom to get through the day. What a relief it is that you can ask for divine inspiration in parenting, you can seek answers revealed from above, and you can knock expecting the door of wisdom will open.

Grace and peace be yours in abundance through the knowledge of God and of Jesus our Lord. His divine power has given us everything we need for life and godliness through our knowledge of him.
2 Peter 1:2–3 NIV

God, thank you that moment by moment I can knock on the door of wisdom and find the answers I need to be a good parent.
Amen.

PRAYER
Reaching for Promises

O Lord God, in whom we live and move
and have our being, open our eyes that
we may behold thy fatherly presence ever
about us. Draw our hearts to thee with
the power of thy love. Teach us to be
anxious for nothing, and when we have
done what thou hast given us to do, help
us, O God our Savior, to leave the issue
to thy wisdom. Take from us all doubt
and mistrust. Lift our thoughts to thee in
heaven, and make us to know that all
things are possible to us through thy Son
our Redeemer. Amen.

THE BOOK OF COMMON PRAYER

No matter how many promises God has made,
they are "Yes" in Christ. And so through him the
"Amen" is spoken by us to the glory of God.

2 Corinthians 1:20 NIV

THE TREE OF PROMISE WILL NOT RELEASE ITS
FRUIT UNLESS SHAKEN BY THE HAND OF PRAYER.

AUTHOR UNKNOWN

Until now you have not asked for anything
in my name. Ask and you will receive,
and your joy will be complete.

John 16:24 NIV

The Spirit himself testifies with our spirit that we are God's children.

Romans 8:16 NIV

The Empty Chair

A church preschool teacher looked at her group of wiggling four-year-olds and smiled. "Today we are going to have a special guest," she said mysteriously. "You can't see our special guest. You can't hear our special guest. But we are going to place his chair right here while I tell the Bible story."

"I know who you mean," said Taylor wisely. "You mean Jesus."

"You're right, Taylor. Jesus is with us wherever we go. I will put the chair here for us to help us remember he's here with us today. We can pray to him just like we'd talk to him if he were sitting in this chair."

He took the children in his arms, put his hands on them and blessed them.

Mark 10:16 NIV

The next day the children again gathered for group time. Blake had been absent the day before and didn't know the reason for the empty chair. He was the last one to sit and plopped down in the chair meant for Jesus.

"You're sitting on Jesus," Taylor admonished him loudly. Blake looked startled and jumped up.

"I didn't mean to."

Taylor thought for a moment. "It's okay," she said comfortingly. "He's waiting to hear our prayers. I bet he just thought you wanted to sit on his lap."

What a joy it is to know that God hears your prayers and that you can talk to him as comfortably as you would talk to a friend sitting beside you.

He said to them, "Let the little children come to me, and do not hinder them, for he kingdom of God belongs to such as these."
Mark 10:14 NIV

God, thank you that you are always near enough to hear and care.
Amen.

Lesson from a Sack Lunch

In the 1940s, not even the city of Chicago knew what a pizzeria was. Sixteen-year-old Italian-American Gina took the lunch her mother had prepared for her and left for work. She was thrilled with her first job at Saks Fifth Avenue but less than thrilled with the contents of her sack lunch.

She dreaded the lunchroom. The other girls had sandwiches made from the new factory-baked bread and deli bologna. Gina was embarrassed to find the homemade bread and stuffed artichoke, or "pizza," her mother had made for her. Whoever heard of pizza except other Italian families?

Gina had no choice. She sat by herself at lunch and hoped no one else would notice her usual fare. It was not to be. Another girl came to sit by her. "Your lunch smells so good," she said. "I'm so tired of bologna. Could I try some?"

*Be content with what
you have, because
God has said, "Never
will I forsake you."*

Hebrews 13:5 NIV

Fifty years later Gina

a friend, "My mother cooked with olive oil, tomato paste, and whole-wheat flour. Now we know for a fact that these were healthier for my heart than artery-clotting bologna. The final irony is that today, 'stuffed artichoke' in a restaurant costs fifteen dollars plus the tip!"

One of the joys of being a child of God is trusting in him. While you may not understand why you face circumstances that seem to be uncomfortable, as time goes by, you may gain a different perspective and understanding.

Create in me a pure heart, O God, and renew a steadfast spirit within me. . . . Restore to me the joy of your salvation and grant me a willing spirit, to sustain me.
Psalm 51:10, 12 NIV

God, may I trust that no matter what the circumstance, you always have in mind what is best for me.
Amen.

Faith by Design

Cindy wiped a tear from her eye. Every time she thought of her mother, she asked God the same question—"Why, Lord? I need her."

During the weeks after the funeral, quilting became a way for Cindy to deal with her grief. Fabric in hand, she concentrated on carefully placing the pattern over just the right hues of color. Every block she made was as therapeutic as it was aesthetic. She felt close to her mother as she worked with patterns and cloth.

Cindy's earliest memories included the humming of a sewing machine. As a very little girl, she had peeked over the top of the table as her mother, Marilyn, cut out patterns and stacked them neatly. She had watched as the pieces came together forming dresses, shorts, and more. Cindy thought all mothers could sew. She grew up thinking that that's what all mothers did.

Her mother had given Cindy a working sewing machine on her ninth birthday. Cindy was thrilled. She spent many happy hours under her mother's experienced eyes learning to sew. A stickler for neatness, Marilyn tried to teach her daughter to keep her work tidy. By the time she was in high school, Cindy had learned to sew well, but she never did learn to be neat about it.

Spending time in the sewing room with her mother taught Cindy many lessons of life besides the construction of garments.

One day, when Cindy was seventeen, she had come home from school crying.

"What's the matter, honey?" her mother asked as she laid aside her hemming.

"Carol is moving away," she'd replied in a choked voice. Carol had been her best friend at school since fourth grade.

"I'm so sorry. Where is she going?"

"California." Seven states away.

Marilyn did her best to comfort her daughter. She suggested that they make something for Carol as a going-away gift. Carol was thrilled with the dress they'd designed together for her.

"I know it's just a small thing," Cindy said to her mother after Carol had left. "But I am glad I could give her a gift that made her happy. She said she would always remember me when she wore the dress."

"Sometimes it's the smallest things we do that mean the most and are remembered the longest. You both will always remember the special friendship you shared. It's never easy to _____ friend. You just have to trust that right now it is God's p_____ pray that God will help you both be happy where you are. Someday maybe you'll have the opportunity to be together again."

Cindy wasn't sure she liked God's plan. Dear God, she prayed. Help me have faith like my mother's someday.

In college, Cindy applied her mother's sewing lessons to a new skill—quilting. After she married and had a house of her own, her mother came to visit Cindy's busy workroom. She'd shake her head at the piles of fabric and stacks of quilt pieces—the evidence of multiple projects and Marilyn's failure in teaching Cindy to be neat. "I know you know what you're doing," her mother teased her, "but how you ever get a quilt out of all this chaos is beyond me."

When Cindy's daughter, Emily, was born, Marilyn sewed beautiful clothes for her. Those happy days were good memories. Now Cindy struggled to concentrate on quilting and tried not to miss her mother. It was painful to realize that Emily would never again wear a new dress with a special tag lovingly stitched inside, "Handmade by Marilyn."

Like a camera suddenly coming into focus, she became aware of her messy workroom. Her mother's voice echoed from a conversation past: "I know you know what you're doing, but how you ever get a quilt out of all this chaos in beyond me."

"My life is certainly in chaos right now," Cindy said aloud. "I can't make sense of any of it." She longed to hear her mother's voice again, explaining that God knew what he was doing and had a plan. Another long-forgotten conversation came to mind: "It's never easy to part with your best friend. You just have to trust that right now it is God's plan for you and your friend to be apart. Just pray that God will help you both be happy where you are."

Mom is happy, Cindy thought. *She's in heaven. I'm the one who's lost her best friend.*

Just then the mail carrier rang the doorbell, interrupting her thoughts. When she went to the door, he handed her a box. Inside it was a dress and a card tucked beside it. The gift was from her old friend, Carol. The note read, "I just heard about your mom and can only guess how much you are missing her. My mother never taught me to sew, but I found a lady here who made this dress for Emily. I know it's only a small thing. But I wanted you to know that my thoughts and prayers are with you. Love, Carol." Stitched into the neckline was a dressmaker tag that read, "Handmade by Marilyn."

Cindy felt like she'd just been given a reassuring hug from heaven.

"Dear God," she prayed through her tears. "I know Mom is happy where she is. Help me to learn to be happy again too."

We know that in all things God works for the good of those who love him, who have been called according to his purpose.

Romans 8:28 NIV

See what large letters I use as I write to you with my own hand!

Galatians 6:11 NIV

Kisses and Hugs

Chelsea shut the door of her mother's bedroom with a happy smile on her face. Kimberly saw her and knew what she'd find under her pillow. It would be a note written with the first careful pen strokes of a first grader. Sometimes a note just said "XXX" for kisses and "OOO" for hugs. Sometimes it was a note of thanks. Sometimes Chelsea sent a note telling her mother about something bothering her. Always it was something for a mother's heart to treasure.

"What's this?" she asked out loud as she found a book made from construction paper under her pillow

Chelsea peeked around the bedroom door. "It's a book."

"What kind of book?"

"A whole book of kisses and hugs written down."

"What a wonderful gift!" Kimberly exclaimed.

May the words of my mouth and the mediation of my heart be pleasing in your sight, O LORD, my Rock and my Redeemer.

Psalm 19:14 NIV

She opened the little book and found two construction-paper hearts carefully pasted to the first page. "This little heart is mine," said Chelsea. "The big heart is yours. I wrote some hugs on your heart. Will you write some kisses on mine?"

Kimberly was only too happy write some kisses on pages she knew she'd treasure forever.

Nothing is quite as precious as a heartfelt note of love from a child. As you write down your thoughts and feelings in prayer, you offer God a special gift. A gift of your innermost thoughts written down is just another way of expressing your heart to him.

You are the children of the LORD your God. . . . Of all the peoples on the face of the earth, the LORD has chosen you to be his treasured possession.
Deuteronomy 14:1–2 NIV

God, I thank you that you receive my every prayer— written or spoken—as a loving parent who treasures every word.
Amen.

Family Picnic

As Jenna reread the story of Mary and Joseph returning to look for Jesus at the temple, she saw the event with new eyes. Just that morning her teenage son, Jordan, had balked at the prospect of a family reunion. "I promised Melissa I would take her to a concert that day," Jordan had explained. But Jenna insisted he cancel his plans.

Why did Jesus not rejoin the family entourage to travel home? she wondered. Certainly rebellion wasn't his motivation. Did a family trip hold less appeal for Jesus than listening and asking questions? Mary and Joseph experienced the beginnings of a transformation in their relationship with Jesus. They began to understand that God had other plans for him than they did. *Mary had to learn to let Jesus go and live the life God planned for him,* Jenna considered for the first time. *Maybe the time has come for me to begin letting go.*

40

"Let's compromise," Jenna later said to her son. "Come to the family picnic for two hours. Then you can go to the concert."

Jordan hugged his mom. "Thanks for considering my plans to be important too."

The teenage years bring changes in the relationship between mothers and their children. With Scripture in hand for guidance and prayer in heart for wisdom, mothers sometimes need to ponder in their hearts that even Jesus' mother had to learn to let go.

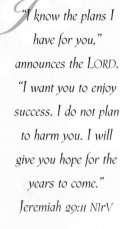

"I know the plans I have for you," announces the LORD. "I want you to enjoy success. I do not plan to harm you. I will give you hope for the years to come." Jeremiah 29:11 NIrV

God, help me know how to learn to start letting go, when the time is right. Amen.

PRAYER
Morning's Gift

Joyful, joyful, we adore Thee, God of
glory, Lord of love:
Hearts unfold like flowers before Thee,
opening to the sun above.
Melt the clouds of sin and sadness; drive
the dark of doubt away;
Giver of immortal gladness, fill us with
the light of day!

HENRY VAN DYKE

42

This is the day the LORD has made;
  let us rejoice and be glad in it.

Psalm 118:24 NIV

EACH DAY IS A GIFT TO BE

OPENED WITH PRAYER.

AUTHOR UNKNOWN

In the morning, O LORD, you hear
my voice; in the morning I lay my requests
  before you and wait in expectation.

Psalm 5:3 NIV

Sing praise to his name,
  extol him who rides on the clouds.

  Psalm 68:4 NIV

Dancing Leaves

It was a beautiful autumn afternoon. Jadine watched as the wind lifted up colorful leaves into a swirling dance and then gently dropped them to earth again. Like a dancer who only lightly touches the ground before making another graceful leap into the air, the leaves lighted for just a moment before being caught up into another twirling movement over their grassy stage. Taking these sylvan moments to heart, Jadine took a pen in hand and wrote a poem:

Lord of the twirling, dancing leaves—they ride the wind away,

On a journey to an unknown place, yet dancing all the way.

All you have made
will praise you, O
LORD; your saints
will extol you.

Psalm 145:10 NIV

Lord of the twirling, dancing leaves, you're the keeper of the wind.

It is you who guides each traveling leaf to places they've not been.

Lord of the twirling, dancing leaves, I'm on a journey too;

44

No matter what the journey brings,
I know you'll carry me through.

Jadine felt her heart lift into a
dance of praise as she sat beneath a
golden autumn sky.

∽

*Serene moments with God's creation
have brought poetry and songs of
praise to many hearts through the
ages. Whether you write with the
heart of a poet, sing with the gifted
voice of a musician, or express your
love for God in some other way,
words of praise are like sweet hymns
to God's listening ears.*

Praise be to the LORD. . . .
*my heart trusts in him, and
I am helped. My heart leaps
for joy and I will give
thanks to him in song.*
Psalm 28:6–7 NIV

*God, thank you for the
beauty of creation and its
power to inspire in me a
heartfelt song of praise.*
Amen.

If two of you on earth agree about anything you ask for,
it will be done for you.

        Matthew 18:19 NIV

Twist of Faith

    Trish and Jennifer were friends. Though they never discussed becoming prayer partners, they just naturally began to pray for each other's needs.

    Trish's baby was due soon, and she needed a baby crib. Trish knew she could probably find a hand-me-down, but she really wanted a new crib for her first baby. She prayed about it and shared her heart with her friend. Though they never talked about it again, Jennifer often mentioned Trish's need in her prayers.

    Neither knew the other signed up for a drawing to win a baby bed in a local store. Trish prayed about signing up for the drawing. She believed that God might grant her request through the contest. But as the day passed for the winning participant to be notified, Trish realized that she hadn't won. She never said anything to Jennifer about how disappointed she felt.

We've promised to be friends. We've said, "The LORD is a witness between you and me."

1 Samuel 20:42 NIrV

    The weeks passed quickly.

Jennifer gave Trish a lovely baby shower. Trish was stunned when Jennifer's husband carried in a box that contained a beautiful, new baby crib. "You'll never believe how God answered my prayer for you!" Jennifer exclaimed happily. "I signed up for a drawing at a store and won."

Two people are better than one. They can help each other in everything they do. . . . And a rope made out of three cords isn't easily broken.
Ecclesiastes 4:9, 12 NIrV

It is an extraordinary gift from God to have a close friend with whom you share your prayers and your life. Who better than a friend to be a witness to an answered prayer? And what a special joy to say to a friend, "God answered my prayer for you."

God, may I have and be a friend who shares the joys of answered prayer.
Amen.

Train a child in the way he should go,

and when he is old he will not turn from it.

Proverbs 22:6 NIV

Growing Sunflowers

Every year, Loren planted a row of sunflowers in her back yard next to the fence. She loved looking out her kitchen window to see their cheerful faces pointing toward the sun.

"Why do you always plant sunflowers, Mommy?" her daughter asked one morning.

Loren considered her question. Was this an opportunity to plant a little seed of faith?

"I guess because Grandma loved them so much," she answered. "She planted them every year too. She said that sunflowers helped her remember she had a special task in life, and that was to raise children who would be happy and want to follow God. She said that I was like a happy little sunflower to her."

The field is the world, and the good seed are the children of the kingdom.

Matthew 13:38 NRSV

"Why?" the puzzled little girl asked.

"Like a sunflower always turns its face toward the sun, she wanted me to always follow God's Son. She wanted me to know I could always look to God for answers to prayer."

The little girl thought for a moment before asking, "Am I your sunflower?"

"Yes, sweetie, you are."

Hugging each other, they stood together by the window watching the flowers bask in the sunlight.

God delights in the good seeds that spill from your life into your children's hearts. And just as the sunflower points to the sun, you can rest in the hope that your children will grow up to follow the Son and someday scatter good seeds of their own.

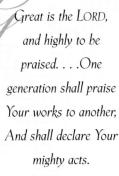

Great is the LORD, and highly to be praised. . . .One generation shall praise Your works to another, And shall declare Your mighty acts.
Psalm 145:3–4 NASB

God, may my life spill many good seeds into the hearts of my children. May I teach them to follow the light of your Son.
Amen.

The Glory Mission

Knowing the skies ahead could be bumpy, Sherry fastened her seat belt and tried to clear her mind for some much-needed prayer. The prayer on her heart was difficult to form into words. She didn't know the problem; her daughter had only said she needed for her to come.

Settling as comfortably as she could into the seat, she looked out the window and saw something she had never seen before. The engines had what looked like a rainbow projected ahead of them. In the center of each rainbow was a cross. Just as she noticed this unusual phenomenon, the pilot spoke over the intercom with an explanation.

"When conditions are just right, the rainbow and cross form. Some pilots in World War II who saw this phenomenon while flying took it as a sign that they were flying a 'glory mission.'"

A glory mission, Sherry wondered. *Is that what I'm on?* Even as the thoughts formed in her head, she knew the answer. Now a prayer came easily. *Thank you, God, for helping me to see that whatever lies ahead, I am on a glory mission for you.* God would use her to help her daughter. She smiled.

∞

Just as the right conditions in the sky can create the radiance of a "glory mission," circumstances in life create opportunities to shine with the radiance of God's glory. As faith in God's promises and love shines from your heart, your life becomes a glory mission for him.

As the appearance of the rainbow in the clouds on a rainy day, so was the appearance of the surrounding radiance. Such was the appearance of the likeness of the glory of the LORD.
Ezekiel 1:28 NASB

God, may I see every day as an opportunity to be on a glory mission for you.
Amen.

HANDS
of worship

Lord of the loving heart,

May mine be loving too.

Lord of the gentle hands,

May mine be gentle too.

Lord of the willing feet,

May mine be willing too,

So may I grow more like Thee

In all I say and do.

AUTHOR UNKNOWN

*Offer yourselves as a living sacrifice to God,
dedicated to his service and pleasing to him.
This is the true worship that you should offer.*

Romans 12:1 GNT

THE MOST ELOQUENT PRAYER IS THE PRAYER
THROUGH HANDS THAT HEAL AND BLESS.
THE HIGHEST FORM OF WORSHIP IS THE
WORSHIP OF UNSELFISH CHRISTIAN SERVICE.

BILLY GRAHAM

Kindness shown to the poor is an act of worship.

Proverbs 14:31 GNT

The land into which you are about to cross . . .
drinks water from the rain of heaven.

Deuteronomy 11:11 NASB

Taste and See

Natalie listened as Daniel described the land he thought was an answer to prayer. His excitement was contagious as he painted a word picture of the two of them strolling through rows of abundant vines in a lush, green valley. Daniel would have to make a down payment before Natalie could see it firsthand. *God, help me know what to do*, she prayed.

As she listened, Daniel's words, ripe with images of gentle showers, sun-warmed days, and a bountiful harvest, reminded her of the story in the Bible about the Promised Land. Because the Israelites knew little about the land God had promised them, Moses sent scouts ahead to a land where a single cluster of grapes required two men to carry them on a pole. The scouts' testimony and evidence of a fruitful harvest beckoned God's people to enter the Promised Land.

Let us continually offer a sacrifice of praise to God, that is, the fruit of lips that confess his name.

Hebrews 13:15 NRSV

Natalie decided that Daniel's testimony was all she needed to beckon

54

her to buy the land. Crossing into their land of promise yielded abundant results for the young couple. Natalie felt showered with blessings and soon invited others to come and taste the fruit of their harvest.

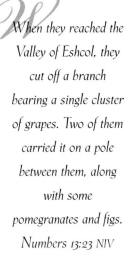

Showers of blessing await you in the land where prayer's fruit grows. Your harvest will become a testimony to the sweetness of God's provision. Like the mission of the scouts sent ahead by Moses, your mission is to sample the prayer's fruit and then beckon others to taste and see that the Lord is good.

When they reached the Valley of Eshcol, they cut off a branch bearing a single cluster of grapes. Two of them carried it on a pole between them, along with some pomegranates and figs.
Numbers 13:23 NIV

God, I praise you that I can cross daily into the promised land of prayer and taste the fruit of your love and provision for me.
Amen.

Freedom's Torch

"I never knew the Statue of Liberty had a full name," Tracie said to her daughter as they waited in line to see New York Harbor's most famous lady. *"Liberty Enlightening the World,"* she read, "was a gift from France in 1884."

"Lady Liberty's crown," Bella read, "has seven spikes on it that stand for the seven seas and seven continents. Her torch shines America's light of freedom to all the world."

Seeing an opportunity to teach a faith lesson, Tracie added, "There is another kind of freedom that shines not only in America but in the whole world. Because God loves us so much, we have the gift of heaven and freedom from the consequences of our sin. Forgiveness is freedom."

In this way you shall . . . proclaim freedom to all the inhabitants of the land.

Leviticus 25:10 GNT

"That means we have two kinds of freedom to be thankful for," Bella agreed. Then she raised her arm with a grin. "Look, Mom! I'm shining like Lady Liberty," she exclaimed.

56

"You're *Lady Liberty Enlightening the World*," responded Tracie with a smile. "And like her, may your life shine bright with the holy light of God's freedom."

Just as the Statue of Liberty shines like a beacon to show the world freedom's light, you can hold up the torch of spiritual freedom. You can enjoy spiritual freedom in your own life and share God's forgiveness openly with others.

In the same way your light must shine before people, so that they will see the good things you do and praise your Father in heaven.
Matthew 5:16 GNT

God, may my life shine your holy light into a world that needs to know the life, liberty, and forgiveness that comes from you.
Amen.

Remind me each morning of your constant love,
  for I put my trust in you.
My prayers go up to you;
  show me the way I should go.

Psalm 143:8 GNT

The Family Key

Frances prayed: *Father, our family has become a disjointed group of people living in the same house. We're all going in different directions and never seem to stop long enough even to have a meal together. Please help us.* As musicians in demand, the family's schedule was too full. Her husband loved their musical lifestyle. So did Frances. But her heart told her they were all about to hit a discordant note.

She tried to talk to her husband about it. He didn't really see the problem.

Make me completely happy by having the same thoughts, sharing the same love, and being one in soul and mind.

Philippians 2:2 GNT

One night their son came home and asked to spend the night with his friend. He seemed delighted with the simple plans they'd made. "Jonathan's mom is renting movies and said she'd make popcorn. Jonathan's dad said we could go to the park and toss a football or something. It'll be fun. They do stuff together all the time."

The meaning of Jonathan's words made both parents wince.

Frances' husband sighed. "Maybe you're right. If the choir is singing in different keys all at once, the music doesn't work very well. Maybe it's time to reevaluate our priorities and find a key that works for the whole family."

Does the busy rhythm of life keep your family from spending time together? Finding time to spend together can be a challenge, but worth the effort. May God help you to find the joy of being a family who knows how to stay in tune with each other!

You must all have the same attitude and the same feelings; love one another, and be kind and humble with one another.
1 Peter 3:8 GNT

God, help our family to evaluate our priorities often and seek your wisdom for our life together.
Amen.

A bird of the air may carry your words,
and a bird on the wing may report what you say.

Ecclesiastes 10:20 NIV

Words with Wings

Laurie faced a surgery that would likely determine whether or not she would live. As she sat alone in her garden praying for comfort, a sparrow flew by. The tiny bird triggered memories of her mother's voice singing an old hymn: "His eye is on the sparrow, and I know he watches me."

As a little girl, Laurie remembered asking her mother why God would keep his eye on a sparrow. Her mother had explained that, unlike a songbird, the sparrow is not a bird that most people enjoy. "The only good thing about a sparrow is that it eats mosquitoes. Yet God made the sparrow, and he had a purpose for it. If God cares even about the sparrow, you know he must love and care about you."

Laurie felt a calm assurance that God had a reason for what she faced and that he would be with her no matter what the outcome.

What a joy it is to find just the right word for the right occasion!

Proverbs 15:23 GNT

Laurie's surgery was successful, and she was restored to health. Now she shares her story with others who face uncertainty. "Did I ever tell you what a little birdie once told me?"

Your children will carry your words of wisdom and faith and take comfort from them throughout their years. Your mother heart can be blessed to know that your words have wings that will strengthen your children long after they leave home.

This is what we speak, not in words taught us by human wisdom but in words taught by the Spirit, expressing spiritual truths in spiritual words.
1 Corinthians 2:13 NIV

God, may the words that your Spirit speaks through me not return void. May they have wings to span time and distance and equip my children to walk more closely to you.
Amen.

PRAYER
When Distance Separates

O Lord, our God, who art in every
place, and from whom no space or
distance can ever part us: Take into thy
holy keeping our friends and loved ones
in distant places, and grant that both they
and we, by drawing near to thee, may be
drawn nearer to one another; in Jesus
Christ our Lord. Amen.

∽

THE BOOK OF COMMON ORDER OF THE
CHURCH OF ENGLAND

"Can anyone hide in secret places
so that I cannot see him?"
declares the LORD.
"Do not I fill heaven and earth?"

Jeremiah 23:24 NIV

YOU NEED NOT CRY VERY LOUD;
HE IS NEARER TO US THAN WE THINK.

BROTHER LAWRENCE

 *He came and preached peace to you who were far*
away and peace to those who were near. For through
him we both have access to the Father.

Ephesians 2:17–18 NIV

No mind has conceived
what God has prepared for those who love him.

    1 Corinthians 2:9 NIV

Heavenly Insight

"That cloud looks like a window," Chandler observed to his mother as they lay on a hillside of soft, green grass enjoying the warm sunshine and an ever-changing sky-picture of clouds.

"It sure does," answered his mother. "Maybe God is inviting us to peek in the window of heaven today."

As she spoke, she wondered what her little boy might be thinking. To a child, images of heaven might be clouds made of cotton candy, stars made of jewels, or possibilities of fairy-tale adventures. Maybe this would be an opportunity to explain heaven a little more clearly to his seven-year-old mind.

If the LORD should make windows in heaven, could such a thing be?

2 Kings 7:19 NASB

"If you could stand tiptoe by a window and peek into heaven, what do you think you might see?" she asked curiously.

Chandler smiled. "I think I would see God and the angels. The angels would stand around singing to him."

"I think you're right about that. But is that all you think heaven should be?"

"No, that wouldn't be enough," he answered thoughtfully.

"Why not?" his mother prompted.

"Because heaven just won't be heaven without me."

Scripture gives only sketchy details of what heaven is like. Heaven is the home of God, the angels, and the saints who have gone there before us. Much about the joy of heaven is left to the imagination, but you can be sure of one thing: it won't be complete without you.

I pray also that the eyes of your heart may be enlightened in order that you may know the hope to which he has called you.
Ephesians 1:18 NIV

Thank you, God, for the gift of heaven. May everyone I love peek into the windows of heaven with the joyous expectation of spending eternity with you.
Amen.

*The LORD is close to the brokenhearted
and saves those who are crushed in spirit.*

Psalm 34:18 NIV

A Very Special Christmas Gift

Rich and Pam planned to adopt a daughter from China. Their older son, sixteen-year-old Mark, supported their plan and looked forward to having a new little sister. The family prayed for a speedy adoption, hoping to add a new face to their family by Christmas.

A week after Thanksgiving, however, Rich and Pam received a devastating phone call. On his way home after a basketball game, Mark skidded on the ice and his car plowed into a utility pole, killing him instantly.

Three days later, on the afternoon of Mark's funeral, the notice finally came that a little girl, Liu, was at last ready to leave China. Knowing that Mark would never see this new little sister was painful, but the family looked forward with joy to receiving the baby girl.

Every good and perfect gift is from above, coming down from the Father of the heavenly lights.

James 1:17 NIV

As Rich and Pam looked into Liu's sweet face on Christmas morning, they both knew the reason why they had such a strong urge to adopt another child. It hadn't been happenstance. Just as Jesus was a Christmas gift from God sent to heal a hurting world, Liu was a gift from God to help heal their hurting hearts.

Joy and sorrow are part of every person's life. But if you look for God's gift to you tucked among the hardship and tragedy you may be experiencing, you will find the joy that he longs to bring to your heart.

You have changed my sadness into a joyful dance; you have taken away my sorrow and surrounded me with joy.
Psalm 30:11 GNT

God, thank you for your gifts of happiness. I know that even in the sorrows of life, you can heal my hurt and restore my joy.
Amen.

Bringing Brian Home

Mary poured out her heart in prayer. She and her husband had just discovered that their son, Brian, was heavily involved with drugs. A straight-A student and clarinetist in the jazz band at his school, his life seemed to be following a track that pleased his parents—that is, until the day they realized that something was terribly wrong.

They noticed that Brian had lost a great deal of weight, and he seemed to be talking incessantly. Over a period of several days, a tale of two Brians emerged as they caught on to his little lies and inconsistent stories. When they finally confronted him, he ran away.

A painful search began—first on the phone, then from house to house as they looked for him. One night Brian's dad, Rick, completely unaware that he was knocking on the door of a drug house, talked to someone who later told Brian his parents had not given up looking for him. Brian realized he'd inadvertently put his father in danger and came home.

68

"Dad, they've been known to kill people they don't know who came to the door," Brian said frankly. "I don't want anything to happen to you."

"You know what, Brian? You're my child, and I was going to bring you home."

Mary prayed honestly before God. *How did this happen, God? Brian's dad and I have been as faithful as we know how to be to teach him what you'd want him to know. Whatever it takes, please help us know what to do to put Brian back on the right track.*

To Mary, discovering that Brian had a drug problem was like entering an endless dark tunnel of despair. She tried to remain hopeful. Though Brian's future seemed dim, glimmers of light shone in the expanse ahead through the encouragement of others.

One day, she marked a verse in her Bible: "I will give you a new heart and a new mind. I will take away your stubborn heart of stone and give you an obedient heart. I will put my spirit in you and will see to it that you follow my laws and keep all the commands I have given you" (Ezekiel 36:26-27 GNT). She prayed the Scripture often, *God, I pray that you will give Brian a new heart and mind and put your spirit in him once again.*

An acquaintance who didn't know the story asked about Brian. Mary couldn't think of one positive thing to say.

Seeing her distress, the lady spoke encouragingly, "You know, Mary, God has a plan for our children. What happens in their lives is not about the things we do or don't do as parents. It's about what God wants to accomplish in them." Mary felt those words were meant to soothe her hurting heart.

Brian left for a drug rehabilitation program. The prayers of both family and friends went with him. It would be a month before they would see him again.

Their first visit didn't go well. Brian stormed out of the counselor's office, leaving his parents stunned. The counselor told them she planned to take him to an Alcoholics Anonymous meeting that night. They returned to their hotel in tears. Not knowing what to expect the next day, Rick and Mary prayed hand in hand during a long and sleepless night. When they returned to the center, a changed Brian waited for them. He greeted them warmly.

His parents exchanged glances. They were thinking the same thing. Brian was smart enough to know they wouldn't let him go home unless he cooperated. The change was too abrupt for them to believe.

Brian sensed their doubts. Then he told them what had happened at the AA meeting. "I was angry when I left you yesterday. In fact, I was furious. I didn't want to go to any stupid AA meeting, and I didn't want to be in rehab. The man who spoke at the AA meeting got up and talked about anger and the road of bad choices it took him down in his life. The rehab program has helped me understand that anger is the emotion that I feel more than any other. Mom, for a moment I had a feeling that it was God talking instead of the man who spoke. It's like he told me I had a choice to make. It was a 'this-could-be-you' moment. I realized I didn't want to live an angry life and asked God to help me get rid of my anger."

That day was a turning point for Brian. But even though there was now some light at the end of the tunnel, they all knew they still had miles to go before Brian could be restored to the young man he had been before drugs entered his life. As Mary considered this, she also felt a sense of calm. If there was one thing she'd learned in the past few months, it was that God was with them. He had carried them this far, and she felt his comforting presence now. She felt sure that God would be with them on the long journey to someday bring Brian home for good.

I will give you a new heart and a new mind. I will take away your stubborn heart of stone and give you an obedient heart. I will put my spirit in you and will see to it that you follow my laws and keep all the commands I have given you.

Ezekiel 36:26–27 GNT

New Growth

Molly looked at the trees in her backyard. With the birth of each child, she and her husband had lovingly planted a tree. Now one of those trees was leaning over, a victim of a spring thunderstorm.

Molly's husband pruned the tree as much as he dared. As he worked, he tried to comfort his wife and Merribeth, the child for whom the tree had been planted. "Sometimes trees do come back," he encouraged them. "Maybe Merribeth's tree will grow again."

"Let's just pray that your tree will make a comeback," Molly suggested to Merribeth.

"Is there any hope?" the little girl asked uncertainly.

"There's always hope when we pray," replied Molly.

Through the next few months the family prayed that Merribeth's tree would be restored. The family's prayers were answered the following spring as a sprig of green sprouted from the bare and forlorn trunk.

"You know, Mom, I am almost glad that the tree got struck by lightning," Merribeth said.

"Why?"

"It showed me that there's always hope when we pray," Merribeth said with a smile.

Molly said another prayer—this one of thanks that both Merribeth's tree and her faith had experienced new growth that spring.

There is always hope for those who believe in the power of prayer. Some experiences offer opportunities to discover how prayers can lead to testimonies. Hope springs eternal from hearts that are growing in faith.

Faith and love . . . spring from the hope that is stored up for you in heaven and that you have already heard about in the word of truth, the gospel.
Colossians 1:5 NIV

God, may my every prayer be lifted with assurance that there is always hope when I pray and opportunity for my faith to grow.
Amen.

People may plan all kinds of things, but the LORD's will is going to be done.

Proverbs 19:21 GNT

Reserved for Bradley

Carolyn's prayers seemed to go unanswered. She had advertised for weeks, but her daughter's car still hadn't sold. There hadn't even been any inquiries.

In a sermon, Carolyn's pastor shared, "If God seems slow to answer your prayers, keep in mind that he's on the move to make things happen. Sometimes he is preparing to meet your need through someone else. Trust that God is moving in both your lives according to his plan."

Carolyn changed the focus of her prayers: *Lord, may the sale of this car help me understand how you move in my life and in someone else's life too.*

Finally, a young man named Bradley called about the car. "This car is an answer to prayer," Bradley exclaimed. He would be leaving for college the next week, and he needed a car. The little red sedan was just the right car to meet his need—and the price would fit his family's budget.

Everything that happens in this world happens at the time God chooses.

Ecclesiastes 3:1 GNT

It all makes sense to me now, thought Carolyn. *I think God already knew how he planned to answer Bradley's prayer.* Her car had been "reserved" for Bradley.

∞

The evidence of God's movement in circumstances may not be clear until the results are known. Who else but God can teach a lesson in patience to one of his children while teaching another to rely on him to supply an immediate need?

The LORD longs to be gracious to you; he rises to show you compassion. . . . Blessed are those who wait for him!
Isaiah 30:18 NIV

God, give me patience to trust that you move to answer my prayers in ways I can't always see.
Amen.

PRAYER
Starting Over

O God, the King eternal, whose light
divides the day from the night and turns
the shadow of death into the morning:
Drive far from us all wrong desires,
incline our hearts to keep your law, and
guide our feet into the way of peace; that,
having done your will cheerfulness
during the day, we may, when night
comes, rejoice to give you thanks;
through Jesus Christ our Lord. Amen.

THE BOOK OF
COMMON PRAYER

76

We, who with unveiled faces all reflect the Lord's glory, are being transformed into his likeness with ever-increasing glory, which comes from the Lord.

2 Corinthians 3:18 NIV

PRAYER IS THE CENTRAL AVENUE
GOD USES TO TRANSFORM US.

RICHARD J. FOSTER

Anyone who is joined to Christ is a new being; the old is gone, the new has come.

2 Corinthians 5:17 GNT

*I prayed to the LORD, and he answered me;
he freed me from all my fears.*

Psalm 34:4 GNT

Trusting Eyes

Two-year-old Kelly was in her mother's lap as they both sat at the top of an amusement park log ride. The ride was just about to begin when Kelly said in a quivering voice, "Mama, I'm scared." She turned to look up at her with fearful eyes.

"It's okay, Kelly. Mama's here," her mother said reassuringly as the fiberglass log moved forward, about to make its first plunge.

Hearing her daughter's trembling voice, Sheila chided herself for bringing the frightened child on the ride. *This is far too intense for a small child,* she thought. *We should have sat this one out.* Then Sheila experienced a moment in time that made her heart sigh with motherly tenderness.

*Look to the LORD
and his strength; seek
his face always.*

1 Chronicles 16:11 NIV

The fear in Kelly's eyes melted away as her trusting eyes met her own. Without a word she told her daughter through her comforting look that it was okay, that her mother was

78

there. Kelly snuggled deeper into her lap and hung on tight.

What a beautiful picture of God's love, thought Sheila. *As our trusting eyes look to him for comfort, he wraps his arms around us and holds us tight. Even when the ride ahead looks scary, he'll be with us to the end.*

∽

There is nothing that makes a mother's heart melt with tenderness like looking into the trusting eyes of a child. The eyes of your own child can give you a glimpse of just how much God loves to see your trusting eyes turn to him.

Surely God is my salvation; I will trust and not be afraid. The LORD, the LORD, is my strength and my song; he has become my salvation.

Isaiah 12:2 NIV

Thank you, God, for the trusting eyes that look to me for reassurance and help me understand depth of your love for me.
Amen.

He lets me rest in fields of green grass
and leads me to quiet pools of fresh water.

Psalm 23:2 GNT

Casting Lessons

Madera picked up a fishing pole and said, "I don't know how to cast."

"That's okay," her mother, Jenny, replied. "I'll teach you."

"Don't you get tired of just waiting for the fish?"

"No," said Jenny patiently. "Fishing is as much about enjoying some quiet time as it is about catching fish. I like just being here with you."

Jenny helped the little girl cast her bait into the water. Madera waited expectantly for the bobber to go under. After a minute, she said, "It's no use. There's no fish today."

"Be patient, Madera. You can't tell what's happening underneath the water. The fish just haven't found your bait yet."

Cast all your anxiety on him, because he cares for you.

1 Peter 5:7 NRSV

In an attempt to keep her daughter busy, Jenny showed her how to cast again, then suggested she just practice. Madera kept trying most of

80

the afternoon until she nearly perfected the skill.

The afternoon passed too quickly for Jenny, but not quickly enough for the impatient little girl. "Did you enjoy your fishing trip?" Jenny asked on the way to the car.

"Well," said Madera, "I like the casting part. But I don't think I'll ever like waiting for the fish."

∞

How willing God's children are to tell God all their troubles. But how hard it is for them to wait patiently for the results of their cast. Although he's invited you to cast your cares upon him, you can also simply enjoy spending time talking and listening to him.

The Lord is good to those whose hope is in him, to the one who seeks him; it is good to wait quietly for the salvation of the Lord.
Lamentations
3:25–26 NIV

God, thank you that I can cast my cares and worries upon you. May I patiently wait for you to answer and just enjoy prayer as our time together.
Amen.

Let us hold unswervingly to the hope we profess, for he who promised is faithful.

Hebrews 10:23 NIV

Hang On!

Her mother hugged her and gently stroked her hair. "You're going to be clingy now, aren't you?" said Megan with an indulgent smile and just a hint of impatience in her voice.

Her mother, Sonia, looked surprised, then laughed sheepishly. "Yes, I guess so."

"You're thinking that my brother just moved out and that I'll be moving out too when I go to college next year, right?" Megan asked.

"I didn't think I was that obvious."

"Just think positively, Mom. Someday you won't have to worry about where we are and when we'll be home."

"Spoken like a person who's never had a child. I'll just have to place you in God's hands.

"If he's half as clingy as you," Megan teased, "I'll never stray very far."

God spoke and it came to be; he commanded, and it stood firm.

Psalm 33:9 NIV

Opening her Bible later, Sonja looked for the promises she'd highlighted through the years. As she reread each comforting word, she prayed. *Soon I'll have to let go of my last child, God. Please help me hang on to your every promise and remember that you'll watch over my children even though I must untie the apron strings.*

⧜

If you haven't faced it already, it may someday shake your world to let your children go. As you pray for God to work in your child's life according to his purpose and plan, you will be blessed to know that God's promises are something you can always hold on to.

"Though the mountain be shaken and the hills be removed, yet my unfailing love for you will not be shaken nor my covenant of peace be removed," says the LORD, who has compassion for you.

Isaiah 54:10 NIV

God, help me to hold unswervingly to my faith in your promises for my children. Thank you for all the promises I have in you.

Amen.

Then Jesus told his disciples a parable to show them that they should always pray and not give up.

Luke 18:1 NIV

Your Heart's Desire

Melanie could see that thirteen-year-old Adam really wanted the kitten. He was polite but persistent. His aunt's cat had a litter, and only one was left. "Please, can't we take her? I've always wanted a cat."

"I know, son, but I'm not sure it's a good idea." Melanie pointed out that their family already had two outside dogs. "Your sister has asthma. We just don't know how she'll respond to a cat."

After several minutes of discussion, Melanie finally relented. "Let's talk to Dad."

Melanie's husband offered similar arguments. Adam was undaunted. "Can't we try? If the cat makes Mallory sneeze, I'll know we can't keep her."

Delight yourself in the Lord and he will give you the desires of your heart.

Psalm 37:4 NIV

Adam's sister squealed with delight when they brought the cat home. Melanie heard her ask, "How did you talk them into it?"

Adam said with a grin, "Do you remember the story of the woman in the Bible who kept bothering the judge until he heard her case? I knew Mom and Dad really wouldn't mind if it didn't make you sick, and I thought if I just kept asking, they might say yes."

Melanie had to laugh. "And like the woman in the Bible, you were heard!"

∽

What a gift it is to know that God wants to give you the desires of your heart. If you delight in him and his word, you can ask for your heart's desire with confidence that he will answer. Even if it seems your prayer isn't being answered, keep asking!

Yet because this widow keeps bothering me, I will see that she gets justice, so that she won't eventually wear me out with her coming!

Luke 18:5 NIV

God, may all the desires of my heart reflect my delight and trust in you. Help me to remember that I should always pray and not give up.
Amen.

PRAYER
Refreshment

O God of peace, who hast taught us that
in returning and rest we shall be saved, in
quietness and in confidence shall be our
strength. By the might of thy Spirit lift us,
we pray thee, to thy presence, where we
may be still and know that thou art God;
through Jesus Christ our Lord. Amen.

THE BOOK OF COMMON PRAYER

I thirst for you, the living God.
When can I go and worship in your presence?

Psalm 42:2 GNT

PRAYER IS THE PEACE OF OUR SPIRIT, THE STILLNESS
OF OUR THOUGHTS, THE EVENNESS OF OUR
RECOLLECTION, THE SEA OF OUR MEDIATION, THE REST
OF OUR CARES, AND THE CALM OF OUR TEMPEST.

JEREMY TAYLOR

You will be like a well-watered garden,
like a spring whose waters never fail.

Isaiah 58:11 NIV

Scripture at Work

Stephanie watched in disbelief as a coyote grabbed her son's puppy by the neck and disappeared with him into the woods. Stephanie rushed after them, following the yelping sounds and warning her son to stay back. Just then the puppy's cries stopped. Horrified of what she would find, she looked for her puppy's body, but her search was futile. She tearfully shared her little boy's sorrow, and then she warned her neighbors to keep a close eye on their small animals.

Stephanie remembered a Scripture she'd recently begun praying to help her cope with small inconveniences: "Our light and momentary troubles are achieving for us an eternal glory that far outweighs them all" (2 Corinthians 4:17 NIV). The Scripture helped her to pray, *In the grand scheme of things, this is a momentary trouble. God, please help me through this sadness, and thank you that eternal glory outweighs my grief.*

Days later, she heard a familiar yip, and her son raced to the door. The puppy just appeared on their back porch. The thick collar he wore around his neck was still in place. "Where have you been?" she joyfully asked the pup as she opened the door.

Praying Scripture once more, she said jubilantly, "Thank you, God, for turning our momentary trouble into an eternal testimony of your glory."

Scripture spoken in prayer is living and active, changing hearts and bringing glory to God as well. Seeing the power of Scripture at work fills the heart with a special kind of joy—joy that demands to be shared. May you pray with the power of Scripture and receive that joy.

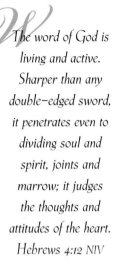

*W*The word of God is living and active. Sharper than any double-edged sword, it penetrates even to dividing soul and spirit, joints and marrow; it judges the thoughts and attitudes of the heart.
Hebrews 4:12 NIV

Open my mind and heart, God, that I may pray the power of your word for me.
Amen.

*I pray that you may be
active in sharing your faith.*

Philemon 1:6 NIV

Stacey's Secret

Seven-year-old Stacey listened in the backseat of the car to her cousin's stories. Her cousin had just learned in school how Christians of long ago had to choose whether they would stand up for their faith or face terrible consequences, perhaps even death.

Watching Stacey's troubled face in the rearview mirror, Brenda thought maybe it was time to steer the conversation elsewhere. But then Stacey's face relaxed as she apparently resolved the dilemma in her own mind. "I just wouldn't tell them," she said decidedly. "I'd just be a Christian in secret."

Brenda smiled at her daughter's logic. To a child, her answer made perfect sense. Brenda resolved to pray that God would teach her that faith is not meant to be kept a secret.

*Your faith, then,
does not rest on
human wisdom but
on God's power.*

1 Corinthians 2:5 GNT

At sixteen, Stacey boarded a plane for Africa. Even as Americans cancelled world travel plans due to safety concerns, Stacey wanted to play a part in bringing other people to God. As Brenda heard her daughter's enthusiasm for being a part of a gospel drama group that performed on street corners in Gambia, she knew her prayers had been answered. Stacy's secret was out.

∞

Prayer is the way to spiritual maturity, to spiritual wisdom and understanding. As faith matures through prayer, the thinking that faith could be kept a secret is replaced by the understanding that faith is meant to be shared.

When I was a child, my speech, feelings, and thinking were all those of a child; now that I am an adult, I have no more use for childish ways.

1 Corinthians 13:11 GNT

God, may it be no secret that I believe in you.
Amen.

In the Garden

Joanne opened the gate into her garden with expectation. The sound of water cascading over a natural rock fountain never failed to lift her spirits. A trellis of roses fragranced gentle breezes with a soothing perfume. As she tossed small pebbles into her garden pool and watched the surface of the water ripple and then grow calm, time seemed to stand still. No matter how chaotic her day had been, the garden always offered a place of refuge. It was Joanne's favorite place to sit quietly and pray.

Prayer is a garden for my mother's heart, Joanne thought one evening as she relaxed in her garden. As she prayed, she spent some time alone with God and her most deeply felt thoughts flowed like her garden fountain. God's love for her and her children was even more soothing than the fragrance of her roses. And prayer made the burdens of motherhood seem more managable—the difficulties she faced more like pebbles that rippled across her life only to fade away. Prayer, like her garden, gave her much needed peace. "God," she whispered, "thank you for both my garden refuge and my beautiful garden of prayer."

Very early in the morning, while it was still dark, Jesus got up, left the house and went off to a solitary place, where he prayed.

Mark 1:35 NIV

Just as Jesus withdrew to a garden to be refreshed, your spirit also needs a quiet place to pray. Whether it's in an outdoor sanctuary or in the silence of your mind before you sleep, spending time in prayer can restore your spirit and refresh your heart.

God, may I find time in each day to spend with you in prayer. Thank you that prayer has the power to soothe and refresh me. *Amen.*

Gold there is, and rubies in abundance,
but lips that speak knowledge are a rare jewel.

Proverbs 20:15 NIV

Jeweled Tones

Jackson and Jerry, engaged in a struggle over a toy, resorted to name calling and then hitting each other as their argument escalated. "Be kind to each other," said Vicki calmly to her bickering boys.

From preschool on, the two boys heard many Scriptures quoted to them. Once Jackson stomped into his mother's room complaining about his brother. "Your brother could use some help today. He was late to his game," Vicki responded. "The Bible says, 'Serve one another.'"

When Jackson and Jerry were teenagers, they asked to stay home from church one Sunday. Cranky from being out late the night before, they were hoping to sleep in. Again words of Scripture were spoken. "As for me and my household, we will serve the Lord," Vicki answered gently but firmly.

Oh, the depth of the riches of the wisdom and knowledge of God!

Romans 11:33 NIV

Gems of wisdom paraphrased

94

from Scripture glittered in many conversations through the years. At their mother's eightieth birthday party, Jackson paid tribute to her with these words: "By wisdom a house is built." His brother added, "And through knowledge its rooms are filled with rare and beautiful treasures."

The wisdom of Scripture speaks for itself. Study it and ask God to help you know which words to use to instruct a child. When it comes to giving wise instruction, all you'll often need to do is share a Scripture. Through the Bible, you have access to all the wisdom you need.

By wisdom a house is built, and through understanding it is established; through knowledge its rooms are filled with rare and beautiful treasures.
Proverbs 24:3–4 NIV

God, may the wisdom of Scripture be spoken in our home through me.
Amen.

PRAYER
A Praying Heart

O God, by whom the meek are guided in judgment, and light riseth up in darkness for the godly: Grant us, in all our doubts and uncertainties, the grace to ask what thou wouldst have us to do, that the Spirit of wisdom may save us from all false choices, and that in thy light we may see light, and in thy straight path may not stumble; through Jesus Christ our Lord. Amen.

THE BOOK OF COMMON PRAYER

LORD, you have examined me and you know me.
You know everything I do;
from far away you understand all my thoughts.

Psalm 139:1–2 GNT

IN PRAYER IT IS BETTER TO HAVE HEART WITH-
OUT WORDS, THAN WORDS WITHOUT HEART.

JOHN BUNYAN

Examine me, O God, and know my mind;
test me, and discover my thoughts. . . .
guide me in the everlasting way.

Psalm 139:23–24 GNT

Learn Things

Judy's eighteen-year-old son dropped her off at work. "Learn things," he said with a mischievous grin.

Judy smiled at the memory from days gone by. For years, she had dropped her three children off at school with the admonition, "Learn things." Hoping to instill a heart for learning, she thought the simple phrase was good advice for a morning before school. The children groaned at first. But one morning her mind had already jumped ahead to the office, and she forgot to say it.

"Aren't you going to say, 'Learn things?'" Adam asked as he got out of the car.

"Yeah," his sisters chimed in. "Aren't you going to say it?"

Judy realized that in spite of the groaning this was a part of the morning routine they expected.

Judy wanted them to learn more than just school subjects. She prayed every day that God would open their

98

spiritual eyes and ears to the things he wanted them to learn.

My son just reminded me of my own advice, Judy thought. *The best advice for a new day is to keep my mind and heart open to what God wants to teach me.*

Every day you have an opportunity to learn what God wants to teach you. An open and teachable spirit is all you need. God wants to help you open your spiritual eyes and ears to something he has for you today, if you are willing to receive it.

Teach me, LORD, what you want me to do, and I will obey you faithfully; teach me to serve you with complete devotion.
Psalm 86:11 GNT

God, as I start my day, may my heart be open to all the learning you have planned today for me.
Amen.

My Father's glory is shown by your bearing much fruit; and in this way you become my disciples.

John 15:8 GNT

Slices of Life

Every Thanksgiving, a variety of pies decorate the tables at family gatherings. Even as families give thanks, taste buds water for delicious slices of pie that are cut and ready to serve at the end of the meal. To many, a Thanksgiving meal would not be complete without a piece of pie! Made of every imaginable fruit, these tender layers of pastry in a pan are a holiday tradition.

Stories from life can become a different kind of holiday tradition. A story about how prayer had made a difference in your life could entice someone who has never tasted of a joyful prayer life to try it. The sweetness of prayer's fruit lived out can be wrapped in tender layers of God's grace and offered as a slice of the Christian life.

With many similar parables Jesus spoke the word to them, as much as they could understand.

Mark 4:33 NIV

As conversations turn to family news this year, there is no better time to offer real-life anecdotes about the difference that prayer makes. True-life stories have more of an impact on others than a sermon ever could. In the midst of your other holiday traditions, may prayer stories that cut to the heart of God's life-changing truths be shared at your Thanksgiving meal this year.

Nothing has the power to change lives like hearing what God has done for you. Does someone in your family need to hear how prayer made a difference? From your heart to someone else's heart, your story may make a difference in the life of someone you love.

If anyone speaks, he should do it as one speaking the very words of God. If anyone serves, he should do it with the strength God provides, so that in all things God may be praised.

1 Peter 4:11 NIV

With a heart filled with thanksgiving, may I share with my family and friends the ways prayer in which has made a difference in my life.
Amen.

Call to me and I will answer you and tell you great and unsearchable things you do not know.

Jeremiah 33:3 NIV

Anytime, Anywhere

In an age of cell phones, it is not unusual to see drivers, busy mothers among them, negotiating traffic and talking all at the same time. Cell phones make it so much easier to carry on conversations at any time and almost anywhere. Calling cards, e-mail, and 1-800 toll-free services make communicating with others more convenient than ever. The art of conversation is alive and well, if the multibillion-dollar communication industry is any indication. Never before in history has communication been so accessible to so many people. Or has it?

Another kind of communication has been available since God created people—prayer. And any time and anywhere you feel the need to talk to God and gain perspective about your children, he is waiting to hear from you. No technology is required. No cell phone or charger is needed. The only calling card needed to start a conversation with him is a heart will-

I trust in you, O LORD; and you, O Lord my God, will answer me.

Psalm 38:15 GNT

ing to listen to what he has to say.

Everyone has access to God. A 1-800 number isn't needed; Psalm 4:3 says, "The Lord will hear when I call to him" (NIV). No matter what is happening in your life, he will always accept your call.

Having a conversation with God and asking his advice is just as easy as calling a friend. Simply tell him what's on your mind and heart. You and your children are God's concern. He can hear, and he can help.

God has surely listened and heard my voice in prayer. Praise be to God, who has not rejected my prayer or withheld his love from me!
Psalm 66:19–20 NIV

God, thank you that I can talk with you anytime and anywhere about anything. Thank you for the joy of knowing that you hear and answer my prayers.
Amen.

Special Time Together

Nathan stood at the library doors, awed by their sheer size. The massive doors were more intimidating than beckoning to the little boy. He took his mother's hand and walked through the doors and into the echoing hall because he knew that reading books meant spending "special time" with Mommy. His mother, too, enjoyed their reading time together. She encouraged the joy of reading in her son.

In the children's section, the walls were lined with too many books to count. The librarian who sat at the children's desk saw the little boy's overwhelmed expression. "May I help you?" she asked.

The little boy replied, "I'd like some books for Mommy's lap, please."

Nathan's mother and the librarian smiled at his selection criteria.

Back at home in their armchair, Nathan settled with his mother for their special time together. Several stories later, Nathan asked, "There're lots and lots of books in the library, right, Mommy?"

"Yes, son."

"I want to read them all!"

His mother smiled. "I'm glad you do," she said. "And I can't think of a more special way to spend our time together."

Your time spent reading the Bible is special as well. Reading the wisdom of the ages may seem a bit intimidating at first. But like a child sitting on his mother's lap, you too can experience the comfort and quiet instruction of a loving parent who longs to spend "special" time with you.

There are many other things that Jesus did. If they were all written down one by one, I suppose that the whole world could not hold the books that would be written.
John 21:25 GNT

God, there is so much to learn from your Word. Thank you that I can spend time with you and read the words of wisdom written for me.
Amen.

PRAYER
Security

Father, let me hold Thy hand and like a child walk with Thee down all my days, secure in Thy love and strength.

THOMAS À KEMPIS

When you pass through the waters,
I will be with you;
and when you pass through the rivers,
they will not sweep over you.

Isaiah 43:2 NIV

GOD IS ALL LOVE, AND THOSE WHO TRUST HIM
NEED NEVER KNOW ANYTHING BUT THAT LOVE.
A. W. TOZER

If I . . . settle at the farthest limits of the sea,
even there your hand shall lead me,
and your right hand shall hold me fast.

Psalm 139:9–10 NRSV

A Divine Gift

Cynthia was exhausted. She had just put the children down for their after-lunch nap and was unwinding from the hectic morning by reading her Bible. She didn't even think she had the energy to pray.

Then she noticed a verse describing how the Spirit pleads with the Father in groans that words cannot express. The passage confused her. *How can the Spirit speak for me without words?* she wondered.

Later that evening, as Cynthia listened to Beethoven's Ninth Symphony, she realized that music can express thoughts and emotions in a language without words. When the Ninth Symphony was written, it was such a new musical form that critics of Beethoven's time couldn't understand his new musical language.

It is the spirit of Almighty God that comes to us and gives us wisdom.

Job 32:8 GNT

Then she considered something else. Perhaps God had inspired Beethoven to create his new musical form. God can divinely inspire prayer just as he can divinely inspire music. *Maybe that passage of Scripture is not so confusing after all,* she thought. If a musician can express a maestro's heart in music without words, perhaps she could understand how the Spirit can express God's heart for her in prayers without words.

God gave the world a new way to pray—a completely new language of prayer. God's Spirit within you can speak on your behalf. It is good to know that God hears the divinely inspired prayers spoken by his Spirit in you.

God, who sees into our hearts, knows what the thought of the Spirit is; because the Spirit pleads with God on behalf of his people and in accordance with his will.
Romans 8:27 GNT

God, it is hard to understand how your Spirit prays your heart and vision for my life. But I am thankful that even when I don't know what to pray, your Spirit speaks on my behalf.
Amen.

Do not be afraid or discouraged, for I, the LORD your God, am with you wherever you go.

Joshua 1:9 GNT

Driving Solo

"I'm not sure I can do this without you in the car, Mom," Katie said uncertainly. "I really like having you there to tell me what to do. Are you sure I'm ready?"

"There's no better way to learn than to try," her mother replied confidently. "You've read the manual and listened to my instructions. You're ready to solo." Silently she added, *And may God go with you to protect you.*

Hands gripping the steering wheel, Katie backed out of the driveway. Pulling up to the first stop sign, Katie recalled her mother's instructions. *Remember to stop completely. Don't just hesitate and drive through.* As she negotiated through the traffic, her mother's words continued to guide her.

The angel of the LORD encamps around those who fear him, and he delivers them.

Psalm 34:7 NIV

"How'd it go?" her mom asked when Katie returned home.

"It went fine. It was amazing, Mom. It was almost like you were in the car. You've been a good teacher."

"Well, sweetie, I may not have been in the car, but my prayers certainly were."

Katie laughed. "If you're going to ask God to go with me each time, I guess I won't ever really be driving solo."

God will go with you and give you instruction for life's journey. His guidance is yours through the Bible and through his still, small voice in prayer. When the Spirit of God is within you, you never have to drive solo.

This God—how perfect are his deeds! How dependable his words! He is like a shield for all who seek his protection. The LORD alone is God; God alone is our defense.

Psalm 18:30–31 GNT

God, what a comfort it is to know that you are always with me. Thank you that your word is my guide and your voice gives me instruction for the journey. Amen.

Sweet Impressions

She speaks with wisdom, and faithful instruction is on her tongue. Give her the reward she has earned, and let her works bring her praise at the city gate.

Proverbs 31:26, 31 NIV

Like many young mothers, Angela dreaded taking her son to the nursery at church. She wanted to sit with her husband and be a part of worship. But Tony, her unhappy toddler, threatened to put a damper on their plans. He didn't want her to leave him.

Angela reluctantly began to peel a clinging, screaming Tony from her side and then handed him to the teacher at the nursery door.

"Don't worry," Mr. Terry said. "We'll have him calmed down in a minute. If we can't, we'll come find you." Angela felt like crying too. Maybe Tony was too young to stay in the nursery. What if he was scared?

"Is it worth it?" she asked her husband. "I know it's the right thing for us to be in church, and I'm looking forward to sitting next to you. But this is so hard on Tony."

"It'll be okay," he reassured her. But Angela wasn't convinced. How could this be the right thing for Tony if he was so unhappy? Maybe they should wait a few more months. She was his mother. Shouldn't she be with him? What kind of a mother was she to leave him like that?

Dear God, she prayed. *Please help us do the right thing for our little boy.*

It took several Sundays, but Tony finally went to the smiling teacher with no tears.

"We've discovered what to do to help Tony when you leave," Mr. Terry explained. "We distract him with a handful of animal crackers. That way he doesn't feel the pang of missing you quite so much." He laughed. "They're messy, but they work."

Thank you, God, that's one hurdle we've overcome, Angela prayed with a grateful heart.

The animal crackers became a beloved ritual every Sunday. "Our Bible says, 'Be kind one to another,'" Mr. Terry said each time he handed out the crackers. "I will be kind by sharing my crackers with you." He said with a wink and a smile, "Crackers help us forget to miss our mommies."

One morning as they were going home from church, Angela spotted a terrible accident on the highway. Several emergency vehicles were already there, their lights swirling and blinking. She prayed for the family of the people in the car. Angela didn't tell Tony why the police had covered the body alongside the road.

They hadn't been home from church long when the phone rang. It was one of the nursery workers. Mr. Terry's mother had been in the accident, and she was gone. She asked that they pray for Mr. Terry. He was devastated.

Tony helped his mother mix a casserole to take to the family before the funeral. As he stirred, Tony asked why they were making food for Mr. Terry. Angela did her best to explain that Mr. Terry was very sad because his mother had died. He would miss his mother because he would not be able to see her anymore since she had gone to heaven to be with Jesus. She explained that they would take the casserole to show Mr. Terry that they loved him. Angela encouraged Tony to pray for him. "You can pray that God will help him feel better."

"Will Mr. Terry miss his mommy?" Tony asked. The thought of a grown man missing his mother was new to him.

"Yes, Tony. Mr. Terry will miss his mother very much," Angela replied. "He is glad his mommy is in heaven, but he will miss getting to talk to her each day."

Together they went to get a sympathy card. Tony, still trying to make sense of all the unusual activities, asked why. Angela did her best to explain that buying a card was another way to be kind and show Mr. Terry that they loved him. Tony seemed to understand, and then asked if he could get something for Mr. Terry too.

"What do you want to buy?" she asked Tony. "How about a card?" Angela suggested.

He shook his head no. He was thinking. Then he led his mother to the aisle where he knew his gift of choice would be.

Later, Tony rang the doorbell for his mother, who was balancing the casserole and other dishes in her hands. Mr. Terry came to the door and welcomed them in.

Angela handed Mr. Terry a carefully wrapped package. She said, "Tony picked this out just for you."

As Mr. Terry opened the gift, Tony said comfortingly, "Don't miss your mommy, okay?" Inside the package was a box of animal crackers. Tony wrapped his arms around Mr. Terry's legs and said, "I be kind.'"

Mr. Terry's eyes filled with tears. With a voice choked with emotion, he said, "Buddy, this means a lot to me. Thank you for being kind to me." He reached over and gave Tony a hug.

Just as Mary, the mother of Jesus, pondered the events of her son's childhood, Angela knew she would ponder this day in Tony's childhood for many years to come. The sweet lesson of how to show love and kindness with a box of crackers had been impressed on both of their hearts. Those months before, she'd asked God if leaving Tony in the church nursery had been the right thing for her little boy. Now she knew with certainty that it was.

Impress these words of mine on your heart and on your soul. . . . Teach them to your sons, talking of them when you sit in your house and when you walk along the road and when you lie down and when you rise up.
Deuteronomy 11:18–19
NASB

Because I Said So

Jeanne was on the phone with a friend. As she ended a long story, she said, "I keep asking God why things have to be this way." Her friend promised to pray that God would either change the situation or change Jeanne's heart.

Later that day Jeanne's son asked, "Mom, can I go to a movie?"

"Which movie?"

He named a movie they'd discussed before. "No," she answered. "No R-rated movies."

"Why not?" her son demanded.

"I set the rules based on what I think is best for you now."

Her son left the room angrily.

The earlier conversation Jeanne had with her friend flashed through her mind like a neon sign. With impatience just like she'd witnessed in her

My trust in is you, O LORD; you are my God. I am always in your care.

Psalm 31:14–15 GNT

116

son, she knew her spirit had angrily left God's presence more than once since the whole ordeal began. With a humbled heart, Jeanne prayed with a more submissive spirit.

God, forgive me for being so impatient. Please help me accept your answers to my prayers because you know what is best for me.

Sometimes you have to give your children answers they don't want to hear. Just as you give your children answers based on what you know to be best for them, God also answers prayers from the perspective of a loving parent who understands what's best for his children.

"My thoughts," says the LORD, "are not like yours, and my ways are different from yours. As high as the heavens are above the earth, so high are my ways and thoughts above yours."

Isaiah 55:8–9 GNT

God, give me the courage to say no when necessary. Please give my children a submissive heart to obey because they understand I only want what's best for them. And help me do the same in my relationship with you.

Amen.

Pass the Salt

Eight-year-old Savannah took a bite of potatoes while telling her family about a new girl at school. She said, "Some kids were mean to her." Wrinkling her nose at the potatoes on the plate, Savannah then asked, "May I have the salt?"

Handing her the shaker, her mother asked, "What happened?"

"We went outside to take pictures. The other girls said Margie couldn't be in the pictures. Margie cried."

"That wasn't a nice thing to do. What did you say?" her mother asked.

"It made me mad. I told them that if Margie couldn't be in them, I wouldn't be either."

"Good for you."

Seeing a teaching opportunity, Savannah's mother then picked up the saltshaker and said, "God wants us to be like salt on the earth.

You are the salt of the earth. . . . You are the light of the world.

Matthew 5:13–14 NIV

118

Did your potatoes taste better after you put salt on them? And did Margie's day go better because you stood up for her?"

"I guess so."

"You sprinkled salt into Margie's day and made it better for her. That pleases God. Do you understand?"

"Sure," Savannah replied with a giggle. "You mean I got to be God's saltshaker."

You are God's saltshaker on the earth. As you go through your day, ask God to help you see opportunities to be his salt in someone else's life. You can make someone's day better through what you say and do. One simple act of kindness can change a life.

In him you have been enriched in every way—in all your speaking and in all your knowledge—because our testimony about Christ was confirmed in you.
1 Corinthians 1:5–6 NIV

God, help me be your salt on earth in someone else's life today.
Amen.

PRAYER
In His Care

O God, whose Son Jesus is the good
shepherd of thy people: Grant that when
we hear his voice we may know him who
calleth us each by name, and follow
where he doth lead; who, with thee and
the Holy Spirit, liveth and reigneth, one
God, for ever and ever. Amen.

THE BOOK OF COMMON PRAYER

When I said, "My foot is slipping,"
　　your love, O LORD, supported me.
When anxiety was great within me,
　　your consolation brought joy to my soul.

Psalm 94:18–19 NIV

AT ANY TIME WE MAY TURN TO GOD,

HEAR HIS VOICE, FEEL HIS HAND,

AND CATCH THE FRAGRANCE OF HEAVEN.

JONI EAREKSON TADA

Even if I go through the deepest darkness,
　　I will not be afraid, LORD,
　　for you are with me.
Your shepherd's rod and staff protect me.

Psalm 23:4 GNT

*All thy children shall be taught of the LORD;
and great shall be the peace of thy children.*

Isaiah 54:13 KJV

Lasting Impressions

Gentle flakes fell all night, covering the ground with another layer of snow. Three happy children tumbled out of bed. "All right! No school again!"

Donna wished she could share their enthusiasm. *Another day of no income,* she thought dismally.

After breakfast, the kids went out to play. Watching them from the window, Donna saw snowballs flying. *Maybe I should join them,* she thought. *They're having a good time.*

The children invited her to make snow angels. Falling backward into the snow and waving her arms up and down was something she'd almost forgotten how to do. As Donna stood up, she laughed with the children at the "angelic impression" she left in the snow. A "choir" of snow angels soon formed.

Our mouths were filled with laughter, our tongues with songs of joy.

Psalm 126:2 NIV

"Thank you, God, for snow and for days off," Donna said.

"I thought you'd be praying we'd

122

go back to school," said her daughter.

"That was before I remembered just how much fun it was to make angels in the snow."

"The sun is coming out. Tomorrow we'll be back at school," her son said woefully.

"Yes, you will. So let's just be an angel choir and shout, 'Thank you, God, for today!'"

Moments of spontaneous, joyful prayer shared with children leave an impression on their hearts. Unlike the figure of a snow angel, the impression mothers leave on their children's hearts lasts a lifetime.

Praise the LORD, O my soul; all my inmost being, praise his holy name. Praise the LORD, O my soul, and forget not all his benefits.
Psalm 103:1–2 NIV

God, thank you for today and the prayers of joy that I can share with my children.
Amen.

He will cover you with his feathers,
and under his wings you will find refuge,
his faithfulness will be your shield and rampart.

Psalm 91:4 NIV

Under His Wings

The banker told Kayla she should consider selling her house or they would have to foreclose.

Kayla prayed, *God, what should we do?*

At home, she tried to cheer herself up by taking the children for a walk. Picking up a long feather in her stubby fingers, her two-year-old asked, "Birdie?" Kayla bent down for a closer look. "Yes, a bird must have dropped a feather."

That night, Kayla sat alone in the porch swing to think and pray. Finding the feather reminded her of a comforting Scripture: "He will cover you with his feathers." The image of God hovering over them and protecting her family made her smile. Maybe he dropped a feather today to remind me he's still here with us, she thought. I hate to give up our nest, but maybe it's time to move on.

You have made the LORD your defender, the Most High your protector.

Psalm 91:9 GNT

The phone rang. "I noticed your house tonight," said the caller.

124

"Would you be interested in selling?"

The next morning, Kayla walked back to the meadow. She picked up the feather and prayed, *God, thank you for this feather. I think we'll keep it to always remind us that we live under the shadow of your wings.*

∞

Small things can have big meaning to a child of God. To some, the discovery of a feather on a walk would be just a coincidence. But to those who trust in God with childlike faith, a feather's timely appearance and the memory of Scripture is a message from a loving heavenly Father.

Whoever goes to the LORD for safety, whoever remains under the protection of the Almighty, can say to him, "You are my defender and protector. You are my God; in you I trust."

Psalm 91:1–2 GNT

God, may I trust with the faith of a child in your love and protection for me. *Amen.*

At Inspirio we love to hear from you—your
stories, your feedback,
and your product ideas.
Please send your comments to us
by way of email at
icares@zondervan.com
or to the address below:

inspirio™

Attn: Inspirio Cares
5300 Patterson Avenue SE
Grand Rapids, MI 49530

If you would like further information
about Inspirio and the products we
create please visit us at:
www.inspiriogifts.com

Thank you and God bless!